MAJOR BATTLES IN US HISTORY

THE BATTLE OF INCHON

TURNING POINT OF THE KOREAN WAR

by Clara MacCarald

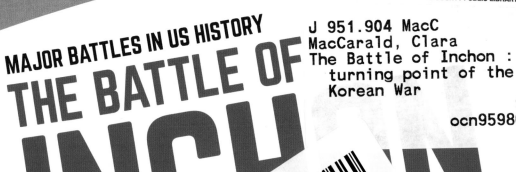

FOCUS READERS

North Star
EDITIONS

WWW.NORTHSTAREDITIONS.COM

Produced for North Star Editions by Red Line Editorial.

Photographs ©: National Archives and Records Administration, cover, 1; Red Line Editorial, 5, 9; US Navy/Naval History and Heritage Command, 6–7, 21; US Marine Corps, 11; US Army/Archive Photos/Getty Images, 12–13; American Soldier/ZumaPress/Newscom, 15; akg-images/Newscom, 17; National Museum of the US Navy, 18–19; Everett Collection Historical/Alamy, 23; Everett Historical/Newscom, 24–25; Everett Historical/Shutterstock Images, 26

Content Consultant: Michael Seth, PhD, Professor of History, James Madison University

ISBN
978-1-63517-019-1 (hardcover)
978-1-63517-075-7 (paperback)
978-1-63517-179-2 (ebook pdf)
978-1-63517-129-7 (hosted ebook)

Library of Congress Control Number: 2016949826

Printed in the United States of America
Mankato, MN
November, 2016

ABOUT THE AUTHOR

Clara MacCarald is a freelance writer with a master's degree in biology. She writes educational books for children. She has also written about news and science for local publications in central New York. She belongs to the National Association of Science Writers and the Society of Children's Book Writers and Illustrators.

TABLE OF CONTENTS

BATTLE PREVIEW

June 1950: North Korean soldiers invade South Korea and quickly overtake its capital, Seoul.

August 1950: The North Korean army pushes United Nations forces into the southeast corner of South Korea.

September 1, 1950: A secret team arrives near Inchon, South Korea, to gather information about the city's defenses.

September 13, 1950: UN forces begin bombing Inchon Harbor.

September 15, 1950: UN soldiers invade Inchon from the sea, surprising the North Koreans.

September 16, 1950: North Korean forces from Seoul attempt to retake Inchon but are defeated.

September 29, 1950: UN forces push North Korean troops back. The South Korean president returns to Seoul, but fighting continues.

July 27, 1953: After three years of fighting, both sides of the Korean War agree to stop fighting.

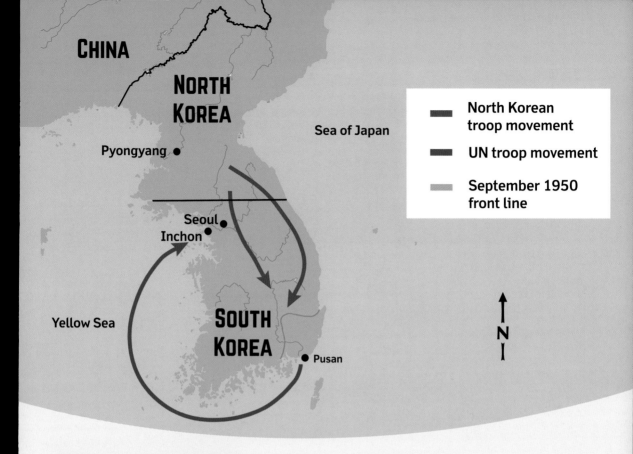

CHINA

NORTH
KOREA

Sea of Japan

Pyongyang •

Seoul •
Inchon •

Yellow Sea

SOUTH
KOREA

Pusan •

	North Korean troop movement
	UN troop movement
	September 1950 front line

N

BATTLE OF INCHON

UNITED NATIONS	NORTH KOREAN PEOPLE'S ARMY
671 killed	14,000 killed
2,758 wounded	7,000 captured

CHAPTER 1

INCHON INVASION

Alighthouse shone in the morning darkness on September 15, 1950. US and British ships carefully made their way through Flying Fish Channel in South Korea. The ships were acting on behalf of the **United Nations** (UN), which supported South Korea in the Korean War (1950–1953).

UN ships sail off the coast of Inchon, South Korea, in September 1950.

The fleet was on its way to Wolmi-do, an island that sheltered the port city of Inchon, South Korea. Much of South Korea, including Inchon, had been taken by North Korean troops. But only a few thousand North Korean soldiers were stationed at Inchon. Also, Inchon was only 25 miles (40 km) from Seoul, the capital of South Korea. The United States and its UN **allies** hoped to capture Inchon and then move on to Seoul.

The ships carefully steered through the rising **tide**. They avoided the miles of muddy land along the edge of the channel that would trap any off-course vessel. The ships neared Wolmi-do.

The big cannons on the ships roared to life, firing toward the island. The battle of Inchon had begun. US planes filled the sky, unleashing rockets and bullets. The North Koreans did not fire back.

MAP OF INCHON

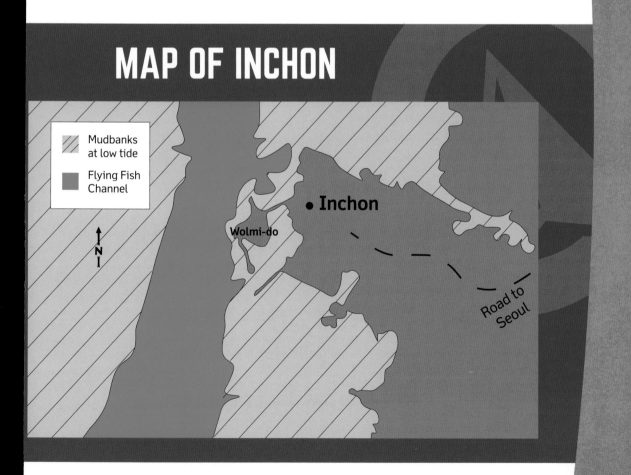

Mudbanks at low tide

Flying Fish Channel

N

● **Inchon**

Wolmi-do

Road to Seoul

They had been overwhelmed by bombings in the days leading up to the battle.

The sun rose. A flag went down on one of the ships, signaling the ground assault. The landing boats swept toward land and began to lower their ramps. Marines jumped into the surf. Tanks unloaded from the ships and drove ashore. Marines swept up a hill. US sergeant Alvin Smith hung an American flag from a damaged tree.

The North Korean soldiers began to fight back. Some threw grenades from a series of holes in the hillside. One US tank shot at them with its cannon, forcing them to surrender. When another

North Koreans surrender on Wolmi-do during the marine invasion.

group of soldiers would not surrender, a tank bulldozed their cave shut. Soon, the marines held Wolmi-do. The first step in the battle of Inchon was over, but a bigger fight still lay ahead.

CHAPTER 2

PLANNING THE ATTACK

Tension had been growing in Korea years before the Korean War began in 1950. During World War II (1939–1945), Japan controlled Korea. After Japan lost the war in 1945, the winning countries split Korea in two. The Soviet Union occupied North Korea. The United States occupied South Korea.

Korean students welcome US soldiers during the liberation of Korea from Japan in 1945.

The Soviet Union and the United States were allies during World War II. But by 1950, differences in **ideology** had made them enemies. The Soviet Union was a **Communist** country and supported a Communist government in North Korea. The United States opposed Communism, so it supported an anti-Communist government in South Korea.

On June 25, 1950, the North Korean People's Army (NKPA) surged south. North Korea's leader, Kim Il Sung, hoped to unify the two countries under one Communist government. The UN **condemned** the invasion. The organization called on its members to aid

Soldiers cross into South Korea. The line between North and South Korea was called the 38th parallel north.

South Korea's army. Several countries, including the United States, took up the call. But the Soviet Union, also a UN member, did not take part. Secretly, the Soviets supported the attack.

While the United States had not given many weapons to the South Koreans, the Soviets had fully armed the NKPA. The NKPA pushed the South Korean and UN forces into southeastern Korea.

US general Douglas MacArthur was the UN commander in Korea. MacArthur laid out a bold plan to retake South Korea. Instead of attacking at the front line, UN forces would invade by sea. MacArthur chose Inchon as the site of the attack. The NKPA would not expect an invasion there. The city was far from the front line and was defended by shallow water.

The planners needed details about the harbor, including information about

Despite the risks, Douglas MacArthur (center) insisted on invading at Inchon.

the tides. The largest landing craft could reach the beaches only during the highest tides. The US military hired locals to explore the channel and spy on the NKPA. The spies' reports helped shape the UN invasion plans.

CHAPTER 3

CAPTURING WOLMI-DO

On September 13, US and British ships approached Wolmi-do. The ships' officers knew the attack was risky. If any ship got disabled in front of the channel, MacArthur's plan could fail. The officers launched small boats into the harbor outside Wolmi-do. The boats carried sailors who could repair the ships.

The USS *Toledo* was among the ships sent to attack Inchon from long range on September 13.

The repair teams carried automatic rifles in case of an attack. Overhead, jets provided additional protection.

As the UN ships entered the outer harbor, a lookout spotted several dark shapes in the water. The channel leading to Inchon was full of underwater mines. The leading ships shot large cannons at the mines. Mud and water flew through the air as the mines exploded. The UN forces then moved on to Wolmi-do, which they pounded with bombs, rockets, and cannon fire. Planes dropped napalm, a sticky gel that catches fire easily.

The NKPA went on the defensive. Approximately 500 soldiers were based at

Wolmi-do, and another 2,000 protected Inchon. The commander radioed to Pyongyang, the North Korean capital.

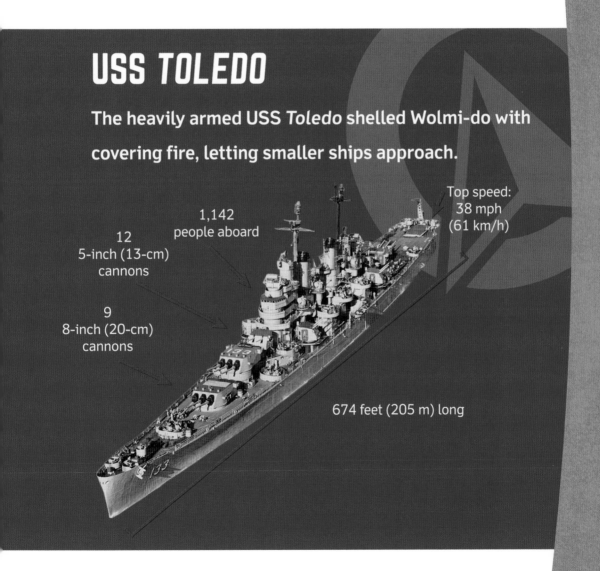

USS *TOLEDO*

The heavily armed USS *Toledo* shelled Wolmi-do with covering fire, letting smaller ships approach.

1,142
people aboard

12
5-inch (13-cm)
cannons

9
8-inch (20-cm)
cannons

Top speed:
38 mph
(61 km/h)

674 feet (205 m) long

He warned of an invasion. But separate attacks made North Korean leaders think the attack would occur elsewhere.

From Wolmi-do and Inchon, North Korean soldiers fired back at the ships with antitank guns and other weapons. The UN forces aimed at the gun flashes coming from shore. The ships blasted these places with artillery until most of the NKPA guns went silent. Then the ships retreated until ordered back for more bombing the next day.

Early on September 15, a lighthouse guided the invasion force along Flying Fish Channel. Ships and planes started bombing Wolmi-do once again.

US Marines move across Wolmi-do after extensive shelling.

When high tide hit just after daybreak, a landing force of US Marines overran the island. They took control of the road leading to Inchon. Engineers laid antitank mines. Then the tide fell back, protecting Inchon from invasion. The next assault would wait for the next high tide.

CHAPTER 4

REGAINING THE SOUTH

With the fall of Wolmi-do, NKPA leaders finally realized Inchon was the UN target. But they were too late to stop the invasion. NKPA soldiers at Inchon waited alone for the second landing of US Marines. While the ships waited for high tide, the fleet and air force kept up the **bombardment**.

US Marines prepare to land at Inchon on September 19, 1950.

UN forces unload on the coast of Inchon when the tide is out.

Then a flag signaled the assault. Landing vessels headed to the high seawall to the east of Inchon. Marines attached ladders to the seawall and scrambled up. Marines also landed south of town and quickly pushed through the city. Ships poured in behind them with additional troops and equipment. The marines fanned out to guard the road leading to Seoul.

A line of NKPA tanks rolled from Seoul toward Inchon. But marine tanks and planes destroyed them. Soon, Inchon was secure, and it was time to push toward the capital. US Marines took a nearby airport. More US and South Korean troops arrived. They fought their way to Seoul with support from ships and planes. Once in the city, soldiers fought in the streets and houses. Both the US Marines and NKPA forces took heavy casualties.

MacArthur welcomed the South Korean president, Syngman Rhee, back to Seoul on September 29. While fighting continued around the South Korean capital, the South Korean and US armies broke out of the southeast, where they had been cornered. They pushed north, driving NKPA forces back to North Korea.

The UN victory ended North Korea's attempt to reunite the country by force. But the war continued. Ignoring UN opposition, MacArthur sent US and South Korean troops north to destroy the NKPA. China, an ally of North Korea, entered the war. The Soviet Union also provided air support to help the North Koreans.

The Korean War dragged on for almost three more years after the battle of Inchon. On July 27, 1953, both sides signed an **armistice**. The agreement created a **demilitarized** zone between the two countries. The border had changed little since North Korea invaded the South in 1950.

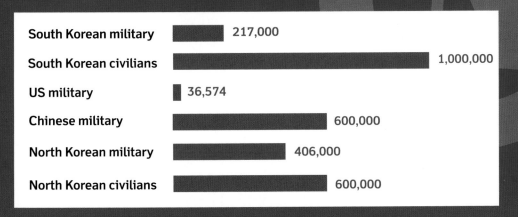

KOREAN WAR (1950–1953) DEATHS

South Korean military	217,000
South Korean civilians	1,000,000
US military	36,574
Chinese military	600,000
North Korean military	406,000
North Korean civilians	600,000

FOCUS ON
THE BATTLE OF INCHON

Write your answers on a separate piece of paper.

1. Summarize the events that led to the battle of Inchon.

2. Why do you think the United Nations sided with South Korea during the Korean War?

3. What was the name of South Korea's leader?

> **A.** Kim Il Sung
> **B.** Douglas MacArthur
> **C.** Syngman Rhee

4. Which of these is a possible criticism of the US military pushing into North Korea after the battle of Inchon?

> **A.** It prolonged the war and needlessly cost lives.
> **B.** It caused South Korea to lose large chunks of land to North Korea.
> **C.** It was unfair to the North Korean People's Army.

Answer key on page 32.

GLOSSARY

allies
Countries that help one another in a war.

armistice
An agreement to temporarily stop fighting.

bombardment
A continuous attack with objects such as bombs, shells, or rockets.

Communist
Having to do with a political system in which all property is owned by the government.

condemned
Expressed disapproval of something.

demilitarized
Having all military forces removed.

ideology
A set of beliefs or policies.

tide
The constant change in sea level.

United Nations
A worldwide organization that promotes international cooperation.

TO LEARN MORE

BOOKS

Bearce, Stephanie. *The Cold War*. Waco, TX: Prufrock, 2015.

George, Enzo. *The Korean War: Showdown with China*. New York: Cavendish Square, 2015.

Perritano, John. *Korean War*. New York: Scholastic, 2010.

NOTE TO EDUCATORS

Visit **www.focusreaders.com** to find lesson plans, activities, links, and other resources related to this title.

INDEX

Answer Key: **1.** Answers will vary; **2.** Answers will vary; **3.** C; **4.** A